LHP

Gina Hall, a Radford University freshman, disappeared on June 29, 1980, after spending the evening with Steve Epperly, a former Virginia Tech football player, whom she had not previously met. Lookabill and his law partner, David Warburton, represented Epperly on the first-degree murder charge, based upon an indictment handed down by a Pulaski County Grand Jury, even though a body had not been found. Credit: WBDJ

"That's a damn good dog!"

<u>Commonwealth of Virginia</u>

vs.

<u>Stephen Matteson Epperly (1980)</u>

A Retrospective

by

Royce Glennwood Lookabill

ISBN-13: 978-1523431960

ISBN-10: 1523431962

Book Design Copyright 2016
Tom Perry's Laurel Hill Publishing LLC

 Laurel Hill Publishing

www.freestateofpatrick.com

Thomas D. "Tom" Perry
4443 Ararat Highway
P O Box 11
Ararat VA 24053

276-692-5300
freestateofpatrick@yahoo.com
www.freestateofpatrick.com

Dedication

This book is dedicated to my loving wife, Jane, who encouraged me to put this account to paper. She was exceptionally long suffering and gracious in light of the fact that when I was appointed as co-counsel for Stephen Epperly in September of 1980, Jane had just given birth to our son, Joshua, four weeks earlier and our daughter, Kimberly, was only three years old. Jane's sacrifices during those months were great and much appreciated.

Dog tracker, John Preston,
and his dog, Harass II, the damn good dog.
Credit: The Southwest Times, Pulaski, VA.

Preface

For several years, I have been encouraged by friends to write a book about my experiences as one of the two defense attorneys in the Pulaski County murder case styled <u>Commonwealth of Virginia vs. Stephen Matteson Epperly</u>. Because it has been thirty-five years since the events occurred which gave rise to the December 1980 jury trial and because many readers of this book, like myself, are not getting any younger, I concluded that the time to write this book had arrived.

In writing this account, I hope to share the impressions of a young attorney (which I was in 1980). The "official" records relating to this case, including the court file and transcripts of the proceedings are housed in the Clerk's Office of the Circuit Court of Pulaski County. It is not my desire to simply regurgitate the contents of the court records. Rather, it is my intent to share the unique experiences which were launched in September 1980 when my partner, R. David

Warburton, and I were notified by Judge R. William Arthur that we would be defending the man charged with the murder of Gina Renee Hall, whose body had not been found.

As I recount my memories of events occurring before, during, and after the December 1980 jury trial, I have fastidiously attempted to avoid any references to discussions with our client which might be viewed as a violation of the sacred attorney-client privilege.

Chapter 1

In Pulaski County, a grand jury is convened four times each year. The grand jury terms are in February, May, September, and November. In 1980, the two-man law firm of Lookabill and Warburton was situated next door to the courthouse on Third Street in the Town of Pulaski, which is the county seat of Pulaski County.

On September 8, 1980, the grand jury concluded its deliberation late in the afternoon. David and I were sitting in our conference room discussing firm business when we saw the circuit court bailiff, Max Campbell, walking from the front door of the courthouse toward our office.

In those days, before the advent of the Public Defender System in Virginia, local attorneys with adequate experience in criminal defense were appointed to represent accused, who were financially unable to retain their own counsel. On that September afternoon, David and I had an inkling that Max Campbell was not about to make a social call.

Max Campbell was a tall Texan who had retired a few years earlier from the U. S. Air Force. Soon after joining the Pulaski County Sheriff's Department, Sheriff Frank Conner assigned Max to the Pulaski County Circuit Court to serve as bailiff for the circuit court judges. He was "all business" and performed his duties strictly "by the book" as would be expected from a career military man. As he entered our office, Max wasted no time in notifying us that Judge Arthur wanted to see both of us in his office immediately. He escorted us next door to Judge Arthur's chambers.

Armed with an indictment charging Stephen Matteson Epperly with murder in the first degree, Judge Arthur notified us of his intention to appoint both of us as counsel to represent Epperly on the murder charge. David and I attempted to persuade Judge Arthur that a lengthy preparation and possibly a lengthy trial could have a significantly negative impact on our ability to earn a living practicing law. With only the two of us in the firm, we had no one to take up the slack in our practice while we gave our undivided attention to this case. Judge

Arthur listened patiently to our pleas, but was not persuaded that our being appointed to represent Epperly would be catastrophic to the other demands of our law practice.

Upon returning to our office, we began discussing the enormity of our responsibilities as counsel for a man charged with the ultimate crime – murder. The absence of a body seemed to make the Commonwealth's job harder and ours easier. Only time would tell if that was true.

Jerry Stewart was one of the psychics consulted regarding
Gina Hall's disappearance.
Credit: The Southwest Times, Pulaski, VA.

Chapter 2

There are two ways in Virginia in which a felony charge may originate. The most common method is the issuance of a felony warrant by a magistrate. The magistrate hears the sworn testimony of a law enforcement officer and/or other persons to determine whether "probable cause" has been established. This standard of proof is applied to the relatively scant evidence presented to the magistrate. In essence, such a finding says that a crime has been committed and the accused is the probable perpetrator.

After a felony warrant is issued by the magistrate, a preliminary hearing is held in the general district court. This hearing gives defense counsel an opportunity to discover the crux of the case which the commonwealth attorney will present to the grand jury if the district court judge certifies the case to the grand jury.

The second way for the commonwealth attorney to proceed in a felony case is to seek a direct indictment from the grand jury without a preliminary hearing or the issuance of a felony warrant. The grand jury meets secretly and calls witnesses to testify about the matters before it. The commonwealth attorney serves as the grand jury's legal advisor although he is not allowed to be present during the grand jury's deliberations.

Because the commonwealth attorney decided to proceed by direct indictment in this case, the defense counsel was denied the opportunity to discover early in the proceedings the nature, quality, and quantity of the Commonwealth's evidence. The only information we had available when we were appointed was from the newspaper accounts in the Roanoke Times and Pulaski's Southwest Times.

From these accounts we learned that Gina Renee Hall, age 18, had just completed her freshman year at Radford University, Radford, Virginia. She had also just finished a summer school class at RU when she disappeared on June 29, 1980.

We also learned that on the night of June 29th and in the early morning hours of June 30th while Deputy Sheriff Bill Patton was making his regular rounds along the New River on Hazel Hollow Road in Pulaski County, he had seen a two-tone brown Chevrolet Monte Carlo parked on the bank of the river with its trunk open. He assumed that a fisherman was down on the bank of the river and that he or she had left the trunk open for the sake of convenience. Some hours later on this fateful morning, Deputy Patton received on his car radio a missing person's report containing a vehicle description matching the Monte Carlo he had just seen. Soon the car was positively identified as that belonging to Gina Renee Hall.

State and local police confer with rescue workers during dragging operations along the New River.
Credit: The Southwest Times, Pulaski, VA.

Chapter 3

Since Epperly was arrested on the indictment, he remained incarcerated in the Pulaski County Jail until we could arrange for a bail/bond hearing. Judge Arthur set a substantial secured bond, and Epperly's parents, Cubid and Esther Epperly, executed a property bond using their residence in the City of Radford as security. Epperly was released from custody after the bond was executed and David and I were relieved that he was free so that he would be readily available to assist in his defense.

Unfortunately for the defense, the Commonwealth Attorney, Everett P. Shockley, challenged the value of real property used as collateral on the bail bond and requested that Judge Arthur order that Epperly be remanded to jail until that issue could be resolved. Judge Arthur granted Shockley's request and ordered Epperly to be returned to jail.

To resolve the issue regarding the bond, David and I contacted a respected real estate broker in Radford and had an updated appraisal of the Epperly family's residential property in Radford performed. This re-appraisal boosted the equity available to the Epperly family to satisfy the bond requirement. Some friends of the Epperly family also posted their Floyd County real estate as additional surety on the bail bond.

Our client was free once again.

David's and my first contact with Stephen Matteson Epperly occurred on September 9, 1980, when he was brought from the Pulaski County Jail to the Pulaski County Circuit Court for advisement of counsel. Once Epperly signed an affidavit of indigency, Judge Arthur appointed David and me to represent him on the murder charge.

Steve Epperly was 28 years old and had transparent green eyes, a ready smile, and a firm handshake. He had played on the Virginia Tech football team a few years previously. Three months later, near the beginning of the jury trial, our client was described by an observer as a young man whom any family would gladly invite home for dinner after church on Sunday.

We soon learned that Epperly stayed in excellent physical shape with regular workouts including weight lifting. He had been employed for some time as a grounds-keeper at Radford University. He also was a substitute teacher at Pulaski County High School. He lived with his parents, Cubid and Esther Epperly, in West End Radford.

Other information about Epperly, was gleaned from diverse sources. From John Buck, the long-time commonwealth attorney of the city of Radford, we learned that Epperly was twice charged for sexual assault. In one case, there was evidence that the woman was engaged in a prior consensual sexual relationship with Epperly. The prosecutor decided that it would be very difficult to get a conviction for rape under those circumstances. Therefore, the charge was dismissed upon the motion of the Commonwealth.

According to persons familiar with the second sexual assault case, Epperly forcibly held the woman's hand over a lit candle until she promised that she would not pursue a criminal charge against him. Since no conviction resulted in either of these situations, we knew the Virginia rules of evidence prohibited the commonwealth attorney from referring to the alleged assaults at trial. That fact gave us some solace.

Shortly after the indictment, I was in the Pulaski County Courthouse where I encountered Don Aker, an adult probation and parole officer. Don initiated a discussion about Steve Epperly concerning some college era experiences.

Aker, Epperly and others from the Radford area carpooled from Radford to Blacksburg when they were students at Virginia Tech. In the 1970's, the route a commuter would take from Radford consisted of Route U.S. 11 across New River on Memorial Bridge to Fairlawn, Route 114 (Pepper's Ferry Road) past Radford Army Ammunition Plant to Prices Fork Road, which then wound through the countryside to the Virginia Tech campus in downtown Blacksburg.

Don Aker related to me that often while they were travelling to Virginia Tech, the heavy Radford Arsenal traffic would force their car to a standstill. On more than one occasion, Epperly would jump out of the car, run up to the vehicle stopped immediately ahead of them, open the driver's door, pull the driver out of the vehicle, beat him with his fists and then return to the car in which he had been riding.

A persistent rumor, that kept rearing its ugly head as David and I were trying to learn all we could about our client's background in order to properly represent him, was that Epperly had been physically abusive to his parents, especially to his mother, Esther. The Epperly family apparently had tried to keep any family dysfunction from the public eye.

A few days after Epperly was indicted, I had the occasion to be in the Pulaski County Courthouse on some unrelated business when I ran into a young woman who served as a juvenile court probation officer. She knew I was one of Epperly's attorneys. As she approached, she remarked that she had dated Steve Epperly. The next statement out of her mouth was an exclamation, "I am glad I didn't say 'no' to him!"

Some things one learns about his client are not anecdotal but experiential. One day David and I were interviewing Epperly in our law office conference room. Epperly was seated near the center of a long rectangular conference table. We were speaking in normal conversational tones when suddenly Epperly slammed his fist on the table. Whatever his point was, he definitely secured our undivided attention. Had the table been constructed by anyone other than my father-in-law, Otis McClung, it would likely have collapsed. (There is a family maxim: "If you want it built to last, get Otis to do it.")

Chapter 4

David and I wasted no time in filing discovery motions in the Pulaski County Circuit Court in an attempt to ascertain the depth and breadth of the Commonwealth's evidence against our client. The Rules of Court for Criminal Procedure in Virginia greatly limit what is discoverable by the defense. Our *Brady* motion for the production of any exculpatory evidence by the Commonwealth proved to be useless in this case. The prosecution had no evidence within its possession or control which might suggest Epperly's innocence.

Realizing our procedural limitations, the defense team set about to interview anyone whom we knew was involved in the investigation of Gina Halls' disappearance. We soon discovered that the commonwealth attorney had advised all the law enforcement officers involved in the case not to discuss relevant facts with us. The defense team filed a motion in circuit court seeking an order from Judge Arthur requiring the commonwealth attorney to cease interfering with our attempted interviews with the law enforcement officers who were participating in this criminal prosecution.

Judge Arthur entered an order requiring at least a modicum of cooperation from the commonwealth attorney and the law enforcement officers involved in the investigation and prosecution of this case. To our dismay, the commonwealth attorney petitioned the Supreme Court of Virginia for a Writ of Prohibition to nullify Judge Arthur's order. The Supreme Court granted the writ and David and I were back at square one.

While David and I were considering how to get over or around the stone walls that kept popping up in our path, our attention was drawn to a newspaper account of a man found shot to death in a pickup truck in Pulaski County on the same weekend that Gina Hall had disappeared. Since we were court-appointed, we did not have the financial resources to investigate and possibly determine whether there was a connection between that death and the disappearance of Gina Hall.

After filing a motion in circuit court to obtain state funds to investigate the death of the man in the pickup, Judge Arthur authorized the payment of such funds in "the ends of justice." We retained the services of Mack Wilson, a former deputy sheriff, to investigate the circumstances surrounding the death of the man whose body was found in a pickup truck near the Claytor Lake exit off of Interstate 81. He finally reported to us that no apparent link existed.

As we explored other avenues of defense, we took the depositions of two witnesses who were with Epperly briefly on the night of Gina Hall's disappearance. We questioned them at length, but both were evasive. Their responses to our questions were slow and well-measured. One of these men was a long-time friend of Epperly. He seemed torn between a concern for being candid and his loyalty to his friend.

In December, 1980, jurors visited the trestle that carries railroad tracks across both the New River and Hazel Hollow Road. Gina Hall's car was found near the site.
Credit: The Southwest Times, Pulaski, VA.

Chapter 5

During the three months between our appointment as Epperly's attorneys and commencement of the jury trial, we filed several discovery motions with the circuit court seeking any information which would assist us in defending our client.

In November, we heard rumors that Everett Shockley, Commonwealth Attorney, might be planning to present tracking-dog evidence at trial. Once again, we filed a motion asking the judge to force the Commonwealth to disclose whether this was true and, if it was true, to reveal the details to us before trial. Our motion was denied and we were left to speculate about this potential bombshell. David and I remained at a disadvantage regarding pre-trial discovery because the Virginia Rules of Court (Criminal Procedure) did not, by their terms, provide us with the tools needed to ascertain the details and critical elements of the Commonwealth's case.

The defense filed a motion for change of venue on November 17, 1980. Our motion and subsequent argument before the court detailed the publicity about the case and our concern about the possibility of empaneling a jury whose members had not been negatively influenced by the newspaper and television accounts of the case. Although he patiently examined our exhibits and listened to our arguments, Judge Arthur denied our request for a change of venue to a location far from Pulaski County. He did, however, take the motion under advisement until after we had actually attempted to empanel a jury.

As the December trial date approached, David and I renewed our motion for a change of venue. We presented recent newspaper accounts of the case and argued once again that a fair trial could not be achieved in a community saturated with weekly accounts of Gina Hall's disappearance. By written order on December 8, 1980, our motion was once again denied.

Chapter 6

When the morning of December 8, 1980, arrived, the prosecution and defense faced the daunting task of jury selection. The defense's initial objective was to demonstrate that a significant number of potential jurors should be "struck for cause." If this had been accomplished, Judge Arthur would, hopefully, concede that it was impossible to seat an impartial panel of jurors in Pulaski County.

If the defense had succeeded in demonstrating to the Court the near impossibility of selecting an unbiased panel of jurors, we would have renewed our motion for a change of venue and upon Judge Arthur's granting our request, the trial would have been moved to another Virginia jurisdiction. Ultimately, the Chief Justice of the Supreme Court of Virginia would have designated the new trial location.

The prosecution and the defense attorneys were allowed to question potential jurors by small groups outside the hearing of the other potential jurors seated in the courtroom. This interrogation process is called *voir dire* which is French for "speak the truth." If an answer to a question raised concerns about his or her possible bias, we would question that person alone in Judge Arthur's chambers. The prosecution questioned the potential jurors first and then the defense had the same opportunity.

Early in the jury selection process, David and I discussed an issue which went to the heart of the process in a murder case. Since the Commonwealth has the obligation to prove every element of the alleged crime "beyond a reasonable doubt", we needed to ask each potential juror if he or she believed that Gina Renee Hall was dead. If that person believed that she was dead, the Commonwealth would have been relieved of proving an essential element of the crime of murder.

Thereafter, during *voir dire* of potential jurors, we asked if any of them believed even before hearing any of the Commonwealth's evidence, that Gina Renee Hall was dead. Not surprisingly, several potential jurors answered in the affirmative and they were struck "for cause" and were sent home by Judge Arthur. Some members of the jury pool whom had been subject to *voir dire* earlier were recalled for questioning on this issue.

On Tuesday, December 9, *voir dire* was completed when a panel of 24 jurors was approved by Judge Arthur. Then the prosecution and the defense, each, exercised its right to strike (eliminate) five names in an alternating fashion until a trial jury of twelve regular jurors and two alternate jurors was empaneled and sworn in by Gerry J. Atkinson, Clerk of Court. This final process for the elimination of ten jurors is called a "peremptory strike." The word peremptory means "not requiring any shown cause; arbitrary." *Black's Law Dictionary*, Seventh Edition (1999).

The two alternate jurors were chosen by lot and did not know that they were, in fact, alternates until all the evidence had been presented and the prosecution and defense had rested their cases. The 14 jurors were present every day of the trial and heard all the evidence presented by the commonwealth attorney. It was not until jury deliberations were set to begin on Tuesday, December 16, 1980, that Judge

Arthur revealed the identities of the two alternate jurors.

Although the two were free to leave at that time, I recollect that

both remained in the courtroom until the jury verdict was

read.

Chapter 7

A jury trial is the telling of a story, often a very exciting one, with the expectation that the jurors will determine the ending of the story with their verdict. The state's attorney, who is called the commonwealth attorney in Virginia, has the first opportunity to address the jury and to, thereby, preview the evidence he or she intends to present to the jurors in their function as "triers of fact." Their duty is to sort through the evidence that is presented and determine what actually occurred.

In this opening statement, the commonwealth attorney assures the jury members that his evidence will prove "beyond a reasonable doubt" each and every element of the alleged crime. Following the prosecutor's comments to the jury, the defense reminds them that the "reasonable doubt" standard of proof is the most stringent of all standards of proof in the American jurisprudence. The jurors are admonished by the defense to listen carefully to the Commonwealth's evidence and to view it as critically as possible.

In this case, Commonwealth Attorney Everett P. Shockley had the daunting task of trying to assure the jurors that the state's case against Epperly would be proven beyond a reasonable doubt although Gina Hall's body had not been found. He had to prove the *corpus delicti* (body of the crime) without a corpse.

David Warburton, during his opening statement on behalf of the defense, related to the jurors that the Commonwealth's case was based solely on circumstantial evidence and that this type of evidence is the weakest of all categories of evidence. He warned them that they must receive such evidence with "great care and caution." He emphasized that it was the Commonwealth who bore the burden of proof during every stage of the trial.

Chapter 8

As a result of the paucity of pre-trial discovery available to the defense in Virginia and other handicaps which plagued the attorney-client relationship, David and I had to learn about the elements of the Commonwealth's case after the jury trial began.

The trial testimony revealed that Gina Renee Hall, age 18, had just completed her freshman year as well as a summer semester class at Radford University. She drove her Chevrolet Monte Carlo to the Marriott Four Seasons Restaurant on Saturday evening, June 29th, to relax after the completion of her summer class. The Marriott, located on Prices Fork Road in Blacksburg, had a bar area with a small dance floor.

Gina Hall met Epperly for the first time in the dance area of the Marriott that evening. He was there with William "Skip" King who was a long-time friend. At some point in the evening, Epperly obtained from King the key to a lake house near Claytor Lake dam, which property belonged to Skip King's mother and stepfather, Ron Davis. Gina Hall was led to believe that Skip King, his girlfriend, and possibly others would be following Epperly and Gina Hall to the lake house. Epperly left the Marriott with Gina Hall and traveled to the Davis lake house in Hall's Monte Carlo. Gina Renee Hall was never seen again.

Upon request of the commonwealth attorney, Judge Arthur ordered a "view" of the lake house for the next day, December 10, 1980. The "view" would also include the route which had been taken by a tracking dog from Hazel Hollow Road in Pulaski County, across a train trestle into West End Radford, through the parking lot of a box factory, across a street, through a car wash and ultimately to the front door of the Epperly residence. (The tracking dog rumors were true.)

On December 10th, Judge Arthur, the attorneys, the bailiffs, Epperly, several law enforcement officers, the jurors, and other necessary persons were transported to the Davis lake house. As we crowded into the house, a deputy sheriff pointed out things to us as directed by Judge Arthur. No verbal comments were allowed. Then all of these participants were taken to the train trestle which crossed the New River from Hazel Hollow Road in Pulaski County into the City of Radford. We were led as a group across the trestle. The jurors would later learn that the German shepherd tracking dog had been "scented" with a pair of Epperly's dirty underwear and had followed the above described route to the front door of the Epperly residence in Radford, sniffed the door knob and planted himself on the front porch facing the doorway.

After the guided tour was completed, the rest of that first week of trial consisted of hearing from Commonwealth witnesses who had any knowledge of the facts or circumstances surrounding Gina Hall's disappearance.

Skip King testified that when he and his date arrived at his mother's and stepfather's house on Claytor Lake late in the evening of June 29th or early morning hours of June 30th, he saw Gina Hall's two-tone brown 1978 Monte Carlo parked near the house. King walked through the upper level of the house. As he passed the opening to the steep spiral staircase, King saw

Epperly downstairs. King recounted that Epperly was shirtless and that he appeared to be drying himself off with a blue towel.

King told Epperly that he and his girlfriend were going down to the dock to swim. Epperly responded that he and Gina would be coming down to the dock shortly. King testified that he never saw nor heard her voice while he was in the house.

Sometime later King looked up from the boat dock toward the house and saw the headlights of a car as the vehicle left the house. Neither Epperly nor Hall had come down from the house to join him and his friend at the water's edge.

On Sunday, June 30th, King and several friends, including Epperly, were at the lake house having a cookout and playing horse shoes. For some unexplained reason, Epperly remained inside the house while the others were enjoying outside activities.

Later that same Sunday afternoon while they were there alone, Skip King and his female friend were engaging in sexual intercourse on the floor in the lower level of the house. At some point, they both noticed that the shag carpet where their feet were situated was very damp. A forensic expert later testified that a four-foot area of the carpet had been thoroughly cleaned with Dow Bathroom Cleaner. The expert witness was unable to identify the presence of blood on the carpet due to the extensive cleaning it had undergone.

The prosecution and defense stand near the Hazel Hollow railway trestle while the jury inspects the site. From left are Commonwealth's Attorney Everett Shockley, John Russell of the Virginia State Police, defense attorney R. David Warburton, defendant Stephen Epperly and defense attorney Glennwood R. Lookabill. Credit: The Roanoke Times.

Chapter 9

Witnesses testified that, even though rescue and recovery personnel dragged Claytor Lake and searched a wide swath on the banks of the lake and of the river, no body was found. Law enforcement officers and related personnel found a light blue bath towel on the bank of the New River. It was located on the City of Radford side of the river. Tights and a jumper, later positively identified as belonging to Gina Hall, were also found on the river bank. Strangely, the clothing was found neatly folded beneath a small tree or sapling.

It was testimony of some of Gina Hall's closest friends and family that she almost always wore the combination of tights and jumper to cover the scar tissue on one of her thighs, which resulted from her having been seriously burned as a small child. She had been noticeably self-conscious about the scars.

It is incumbent upon the prosecuting attorney in a murder case where a body has not been found, to establish that the alleged victim was, in fact, deceased. Everett Shockley proceeded to call witnesses to establish the normal habits of Gina Hall which would, he hoped, exclude the possibility that she would go on a trip without notifying her sister, Dlana, or her parents or close friends.

Dlana and several of Gina's friends testified, unequivocally, that Gina would never have gone out of town to any secret location without first informing her sister, a friend, or another family member.

Dlana testified that on Saturday night, June 29th, Gina called her late in the evening to inform her that she was at a house on Claytor Lake with a guy named Steve. She related to the jury that Gina's voice seemed to reflect some apprehension or fear.

Ninety-seven pieces of forensic evidence introduced into evidence at trial such as hair, blood, and fiber analyses failed to link Epperly in any significant way to Gina Hall's disappearance or death.

John Preston, a professional dog handler from Ohio, was called as a Commonwealth witness. Preston's $22,000 German shepherd, Harass II, had tracked Epperly's scent to his parents' house in West End Radford, as previously described. David Warburton handled the cross-examination of Preston. David's questioning was extensive and often arduous.

David did a yeoman's job in attempting to impeach Preston's testimony and to plant seeds of doubt in the jurors' minds about the ability of a dog to effectively track a person's scent across a railroad trestle, through several properties, including a car wash and ultimately to the front door of the Epperly house. This feat had allegedly been accomplished ten days after Gina Hall's disappearance. During that period of time, more than four inches of rain had fallen in that area.

David and I had previously filed motions to exclude any dog-tracking evidence, citing factually similar cases from several states. Although we argued that such evidence was unreliable and prejudicial, Judge Arthur rejected our arguments and denied our motions. Judge Arthur's position was that the jury was entitled to give the dog-tracking testimony such weight as it deemed fit. Judge Arthur believed that the jury, as triers of fact, could determine whether such

evidence had probative value. [1]

---

[1] Upon direct appeal to the Supreme Court of Virginia, habeas corpus petition
to the Supreme Court of Virginia and habeas corpus petition to the Federal
District Court for the Western District of Virginia, these appellate courts
ruled, in essence, that although the dog-tracking evidence probably should
not have been admitted into evidence, its admission was harmless error in
light of the other evidence in the case.

Chapter 10

Some of the most damning testimony presented to the jury came from the mouth of Virginia State Trooper, C. Austin Hall. Trooper Hall was not an investigator, but because of his proximity to the location of events of June 29, 1980, and other unique circumstances, he was requested by Everett Shockley to talk to Epperly about Gina Hall's disappearance.

Trooper Hall met with Epperly on several occasions and established a rapport with him. From the witness stand, Trooper Hall related to the jury that he had told Epperly that the German shepherd had tracked him across the trestle from Hazel Hollow Road (in Pulaski County) into the West End of Radford City, and ultimately, to the front door of Epperly's residence.

From the beginning, Epperly had told Trooper Hall that Gina Hall had driven the Monte Carlo from the Davis cabin on Claytor Lake to Epperly's house in Radford, dropped him off there and drove away. When her car was found along the New River on Hazel Hollow Road in Pulaski County, the driver's seat had been pushed back as far as it would go. Witnesses verified that Gina Hall was barely five feet tall. The jurors could see that Epperly was over six feet in height.

During this phase of the Commonwealth's case, the testimony of law enforcement officers was presented regarding the recovery of Gina Hall's purse and its contents. These items were found several yards from the unlocked car. A well-known thief, Jerry Eugene Ross, was interrogated by the Pulaski County Sheriff's Department, and he confessed to burglarizing the Monte Carlo. Although he admitted to stealing the purse, there was no evidence that he had moved the driver's seat or that he had any connection to Gina Hall's disappearance. Upon rigorous cross examination of the officer, we could not establish that there was a possible link between Ross and Gina Hall.

Trooper Hall further testified that back in July the German shepherd picked out the blue towel found on the bank of the New River from among several other towels placed in a row on the ground outside the police station in the City of Radford. The dog then walked over to where Epperly was sitting in the police station, sniffed him, thus linking him to the blue towel. After being told of the dog's actions regarding both the towel identification and his tracking Epperly's scent from below the train trestle in Pulaski County to Epperly's home in the City of Radford, Epperly said with considerable emotion, "That's a damn good dog. That's a damn good dog. That's a damn good dog."

During further direct examination, Trooper Hall testified that during one of his encounters with Epperly, he told Epperly that he knew Epperly had killed Gina Hall and that her family wanted more than anything else to have her body returned to them for burial. Trooper Hall assured Epperly that he had the authority of the commonwealth attorney to offer him a twenty-year sentence for second-degree murder in exchange for Epperly's disclosing the location of Gina Hall's body. According to Trooper Hall's testimony, this discussion with Epperly occurred a few days after Gina Hall's disappearance, but some seven or eight weeks before the

Pulaski County Grand Jury handed down a direct indictment for murder against Epperly.

Upon further examination by the commonwealth attorney, Trooper hall quoted Epperly, in response to the offer to produce the body of Gina Hall in exchange for a second-degree murder plea and twenty-year prison sentence, as saying, "I'll have to think about it." Epperly never got back to Trooper Hall with his response to the proposal.

By the conclusion of Trooper Hall's testimony there was, in my opinion, an obvious change in the demeanor of the jurors. Early in the trial, the members of the jury, almost to the person, looked at Epperly with sympathetic eyes as if they were thinking, "How could a charming, polite, handsome, young man such as you commit such a heinous act?" With Epperly's incriminating statements inserted into the growing body of the Commonwealth's evidence, the jurors' expressions had become hard and unsympathetic.

Chapter 11

By the beginning of the second week of the trial, the tension in the courtroom was almost palpable. That Monday morning, December 15th, David and I made a motion, which we argued in Judge Arthur's chambers, to exclude the testimony of Patricia Hamby, a forensic scientist, who was trained as a blood-splattering expert. She had completed her training in this specialized area, but had not yet received her certificate of completion from the Federal Bureau of Investigation. Out of an abundance of caution, Judge Arthur excluded her testimony from consideration of the jury lest error be interjected into the case in the event of an appeal. Had she testified, the witness would have testified about the tiny specks of blood found on golf shoes and on a storage cabinet in the Davis lake house. During her testimony she would have estimated the pounds-per-square-inch force needed to be applied by one human on another to generate these sub-droplets of blood and that the blood specks were consistent with Gina Hall's blood type.

During the morning's proceedings one of the courtroom bailiffs brought to the defense counsel table a small piece of yellow paper ostensibly torn from the corner of a legal pad. Although, I do not remember the exact wording, the note in effect said, "If Epperly is acquitted, he will die and you better be careful." David and I looked at each other, shrugged, and continued our cross examination until lunch recess.

When the Court announced the noon recess, David and I exited the back door of the courthouse with Epperly walking between us. Although, it was mid-December, the noon temperature was about 75 degrees. As the three of us were stepping out into the alley way between the "new" Courthouse and the historic Courthouse, we were removing our suit coats and laughing about something as a means of releasing the stress we felt from the morning trial proceedings.

Since our law office was immediately adjacent to the courthouse, David and I, with Epperly still between us, walked toward the back door of our office building. We planned to have lunch delivered to our office to give us more preparation time for the afternoon court session. As we approached the back door of our office, we noticed that Keith Humphry, evening news anchor for WDBJ-TV Channel 7 in Roanoke, Virginia, was standing between us and the back door of our office. It was not our intention to grant an interview with Humphry, who had his cameraman and microphone ready for that possibility.

Just as we began to circumvent Humphry and his cameraman to enter our law office, we saw to our left two African-Americans walking toward us along the sidewalk located in front of the Crowell, Nuchols, Layman, and Aust Law Offices. As the two men came to within 35 to 40 feet of us, we saw that they both were wearing long wool overcoats (in 75-degree weather!). We simultaneously noticed that each man was carrying what appeared to be a sawed-off shotgun concealed under his coat.

Commonwealth Attorney Everett Shockley, who was walking slightly ahead of us toward his car, bolted in front of the WDBJ Television camera. David's and my administrative assistant, Ramona Mottesheard (now Palmer) ran to the back door of our office, key in hand, and unlocked the door. David, Epperly, and I literally dived inside our office building slamming the door behind us.

Three minutes earlier, there had been at least thirty-five armed law enforcement officers in a position to assist and protect us. Unfortunately, they were on their way to lunch and not readily available at this critical moment. Once inside our offices, we called 911. It took several officers only a few minutes to surround the Courthouse Square which included our office.

After several police officers performed a thorough search of the area around the courthouse, we were notified by one of the deputy sheriffs that the two men could not be found. Needless to say, after this incident, David and I became much more aware of our surroundings as we carried out our trial duties.

Out of abundance of caution, I carried a loaded revolver in my brief case the next day. It did not give me the peace of mind I expected. In fact, I was fearful every moment I might drop my briefcase and accidentally discharge the loaded Smith & Wesson. Thereafter, I left the pistol at home and relied on the good offices of the armed court bailiffs.

Judge R. William Arthur gestures as he instructs jurors outside
Stephen Epperly's home. Dec. 10, 1980.
Credit: The Roanoke Times.

Chapter 12

After our brief brush with death, David and I thought that things would get calmer and saner. In the early afternoon of December 15th, Epperly requested a hearing in the judge's chambers. The request was granted and the defense attorneys and Everett Shockley joined Epperly in Judge Arthur's office. Epperly presented a letter to the judge requesting that David and I be relieved as his counsel and that a mistrial be declared. The letter contained a laundry list of things that we had not done properly or to his satisfaction and things that we did not do that he felt we should have done. These complaints came as no surprise to us in light of all that was at stake for our client. Judge Arthur disagreed with his allegations, denied his motions, and adjourned court for the day.

There was nothing that could have prepared defense counsel for what happened on Tuesday, December 16. Commonwealth Attorney Shockley called the last witness for the prosecution. When Bill Cranwell was called to the stand

and was administered his oath by Gerry Atkinson, Clerk of Court, David and I looked at each other quizzically. Neither of us had the slightest idea why Mr. Cranwell was present at this trial as a witness. Under the provisions of the Virginia Supreme Court Rules of Court for Criminal Proceedings, we had no way of discovering from the Commonwealth, prior to trial, the existence of this witness.

Bill Cranwell's testimony caused the Commonwealth's case to end with a bang rather than a whimper. He was a Blacksburg businessman and brother of Richard (Dickie) Cranwell, attorney and long-time member of the Virginia House of Delegates. This witness responded calmly to Shockley's direct examination and revealed to the jury the following:

Sometime prior to Epperly's direct indictment by the Pulaski County Grand Jury, Epperly had gone by Bill Cranwell's office in Blacksburg. He and the Cranwells had known each other for several years. Epperly stuck his head through the doorway and asked Bill Cranwell, "Bill, will you ask your brother, Dickie, what will happen to me if they don't find the body?"

The greatest irony in this trial was revealed in the testimony of Bill Cranwell. In the 1950's, he and John Hall, of Wise County, Virginia, were roommates at Virginia Tech. That same John Hall had been sitting in the courtroom gallery every day of the trial of his daughter's alleged killer.

At the conclusion of Bill Cranwell's testimony, the Commonwealth rested her case. The defense counsel made our motion to strike the Commonwealth's evidence, which motion was denied.

The defense team chose to rest our case without presenting witnesses. After consultation with our client, Steve Epperly made the decision not to testify.

Gina Hall borrowed her sister's Chevrolet Monte Carlo to drive to Blacksburg the night she disappeared. The car was later found abandoned beside the New River.
Credit: The Southwest Times, Pulaski, VA.

Chapter 13

After two full days of jury selection, a view of the site of the alleged homicide by the jury, the state's presentation of some 97 articles of forensic evidence, direct examination and cross-examination of lay and expert witnesses, legal arguments over the admissibility of evidence, and dealing with seemingly unending surprises inside and outside the courtroom, the denouement of this drama consisted of the closing arguments of attorneys and the deliberation and final verdict of the jury.

At our lunch recess on Tuesday, December 16th, Epperly insisted that I make the closing argument for the defense. I preferred that David make the closing argument to the jury since he had ably presented the opening statement. He had reminded the jury of the Commonwealth's duty to prove every element of the alleged crime beyond a reasonable doubt. We felt that the jury would rather hear a closing from the same attorney who spoke to them at the beginning of the trial. However, in these critical matters, the client is the boss. So I spent the noon recess summarizing my closing argument on a legal pad.

The jury trial reconvened in the early afternoon of the 16th. After the first part of Everett Shockley's closing argument to the jury, I stood to present the closing argument for the defense. Trying to follow my written notes proved futile. I laid my written notes aside and embarked upon the task of using my memory to review the evidence in the light most favorable to the accused.

I attempted to persuade the jurors that Epperly's statements and actions after June 29, 1980, could be interpreted in ways that were consistent with innocence rather than guilt. Needless to say, it was a challenge to strive to create doubt in the jurors' minds about the efficacy of the Commonwealth's body of evidence. In concluding my closing argument, I entreated the jury to make a finding that the Commonwealth had failed in her burden of proof and to, thus, find Epperly not guilty of the murder charge.

The Commonwealth always has the last word in closing arguments to the jury. After attempting to rebut my arguments and reviewing again the Commonwealth's evidence, Everett Shockley asked for a finding of guilt and a sentence of life in prison.

Although it seemed like an eternity, the jurors concluded their deliberations by late afternoon and returned to the courtroom with the following verdict which read as follows: "We, the jury, find the defendant, Stephen Matteson Epperly, guilty of first degree murder, as charged in the indictment, and fix his punishment at life imprisonment. Signed J. M. Brown, Foreman"

The jurors were polled individually and each juror confirmed that he or she agreed with and joined in the verdict. Epperly voiced his desire to appeal the conviction to the Supreme Court of Virginia. Judge Arthur denied bond and remanded him to jail pending his sentencing hearing.

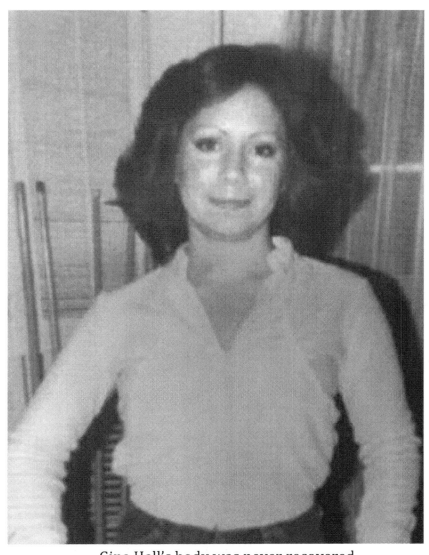
Gina Hall's body was never recovered.
Credit: WBDJ

Chapter 14

On Friday, December 19, 1980, David and I appeared in the Pulaski County Circuit Court for the sentencing hearing. We renewed our motion to set aside the jury verdict as contrary to the law and evidence. Judge Arthur overruled our motion. Epperly waived the preparation of a pre-sentence report and the judge sentenced him to life in prison. Epperly was remanded to the Pulaski County Jail pending transfer to the Virginia State Penitentiary.

The following week, Judge Arthur relieved David and me as counsel for Epperly, and appointed Max Jenkins and R. Keith Neely as counsel to perfect an appeal of the conviction to the Supreme Court of Virginia. In light of Epperly's letter to Judge Arthur regarding his dissatisfaction with our representation, Judge Arthur had little choice but to take this action. By having new counsel on appeal, Epperly would be allowed to raise the issue of "ineffective assistance of counsel" on direct appeal instead of on a separate *habeas corpus* petition.

After leaving Judge Arthur's chambers and being free from any appellate obligations in regard to this case, David and I looked at each other as if asking "what is a normal routine and how do we get back to it?" What had become "normal" for more than three months was now surreal.

We had almost grown accustomed to late night calls from people as far away as San Francisco claiming to have seen Gina Hall on the street. In addition, several calls were made to professional dog handlers across the country to obtain information and, hopefully witnesses, to counter the Commonwealth's forthcoming tracking-dog evidence. Several calls were made to professional dog handlers across the country. All handlers with whom we spoke had had experience with bloodhounds, but knew nothing about German shepherds.

These were but two examples of the many unique interactions and experiences which we weathered during those pressure-filled months. Returning to "normal" was very difficult for me as I know it was for my partner. I was emotionally exhausted and, at the same time, anxious to get back to the routine which had existed for me prior to September 8, 1980, when Stephen Matteson Epperly was indicted for murder.

A few weeks after our duties in this case were completed, David and I each received a check from the Commonwealth of Virginia for $400 to compensate us for three months of preparation and a two-week jury trial. In contrast, our investigator was paid $600 for three days of work.

These months were particularly difficult for me because I was able to spend little quality time with my wife, three-year-old daughter and newborn son. I only hope these challenges were character builders for our family.

Dog tracker, John Preston.
Credit: The Southwest Times, Pulaski, VA.

Chapter 15

Anyone who has practiced law (or watched Law and Order) on television knows that a murder conviction is not the end of the case. Attorneys Jenkins and Neeley pursued a direct appeal in this case to the Supreme Court of Virginia. In his 21-page opinion, Justice Charles S. Russell, writing for the Court, affirmed the conviction in Epperly v. Commonwealth, 224Va.214, 294 S.E. 2nd 882 (1982). On Page 20 of his opinion, after spending 19 pages reviewing the evidence in great detail and the constitutional issues assigned as error by Epperly's appellate attorneys, Justice Russell stated that David and I provided Epperly "an energetic and effective representation."

Some years after Justice Russell's opinion in this case was rendered, David Warburton and I encountered him at the Bull & Bear Club in Richmond, Virginia, at the annual reception we former law clerks held in honor of the Justices of the Supreme Court of Virginia. David said to Justice Russell as he shook his hand, "I'm Mr. Energetic," and nodding toward me, "and this is Mr. Effective." Without missing a beat, Justice Russell replied, "The Epperly case." We each smiled in acknowledgement.

After the Supreme Court of Virginia upheld his conviction, Epperly filed a petition for a writ of *habeas corpus* in the United States District Court for the Western District of Virginia. A *habeas corpus* proceeding is a challenge to the petitioner's detention alleging that some constitutional right has been violated. The Latin phrase *habeas corpus* translates, "that you have the body." The petition was summarily dismissed since Epperly had not exhausted his state remedies as a required by law.

Thereafter, Epperly filed another petition for a writ of *habeas corpus.* This time the proceeding was instituted in the Circuit Court of Pulaski County. An evidentiary hearing was held before Judge Duane E. Mink. At this hearing, David and I were required to be present and we were represented by James Kulp from the Virginia Attorney General's Office. Epperly's attorneys at this hearing were Max Jenkins of

Radford, Virginia, and Stephen A. Saltzburg, professor at the University of Virginia Law School.

Epperly's attorneys at this hearing had summoned a well-known criminal defense attorney from the Roanoke area to testify as an expert about the quality of our representation of Epperly in the murder case. At one point in his testimony, the attorney (who is now deceased) went into substantial detail about several conversations he had had with David and me after we were appointed to represent Epperly. He testified that he had given us valuable advice about how to best represent his former client, Epperly. The attorney then stated that he could not understand why we did not follow his advice.

As the attorney testified, David and I looked at each other with more than a little shock. We both knew, without question, that there had been only one telephone conversation with this lawyer. Shortly after we had been appointed as Epperly's counsel in September, we received a call from this attorney who told us that he had represented Epperly on previous sexual assault charges. This time, the Epperly family could not raise the $50,000 retainer fee for him to represent Epperly on the murder charge. He then wished us well and hung up. We had no other discussions with the attorney about the murder case, much less received any advice from him.

At counsel table during this hearing I sat between my partner and Jim Kulp. The "expert" witness continued to expound upon the advice he had given us about our representation of Epperly. His testimony, as the expression goes "was cut from whole cloth." The conversations about which he testified simply never took place.

I was not conscious of the anger which was building up inside of me as I listened to his fabrications. Nor was I aware of my actions as I rose from my seat at counsel table and began to climb over the counsel table to get to the witness. Thankfully, David and Jim Kulp responded immediately to my actions by each grabbing my belt and yanking me back into my seat. Although this happened some 35 years ago, I am still embarrassed by my actions in court that day. However, this incident did make me appreciate how witnesses and litigants feel when they have to endure perjured testimony without opening their mouths.

As the conclusion of the evidentiary hearing, the *habeas corpus* petition was dismissed by Judge Mink. As expected, the denial of *habeas* relief was appealed to the Supreme Court of Virginia.

The Supreme Court of Virginia granted an appeal from Judge Mink's decision to dismiss the petition for a writ of *habeas corpus*. On March 4, 1988, in a 14-page opinion, Justice Richard H. Poff (formerly U.S. Congressman) carefully reviewed the evidence from the jury trial as well as all the constitutional claims raised by Epperly.

In the penultimate paragraph of his opinion, Justice Poff faulted Epperly for not sharing with his defense counsel before trial the incriminating statements he had made to law enforcement officers and to Bill Cranwell. The gist of Justice Poff's opinion was that trial counsel was handicapped by Epperly's unwillingness to be honest with us. Our status of "energetic and effective" remained unscathed.

Attorney Glennwood Lookabill (right) walking ahead of his client Stephen Epperly (second from right, light suit), leads jury and court officials past the railroad trestle under which Gina Hall's car was found. Dec. 11, 1980.
Credit: The Roanoke Times.

Chapter 16

Since 1980, Epperly has filed other petitions for *habeas corpus* relief, but ultimately all these petitions have been dismissed. He has also had several parole hearings over the years, but has never been released on parole. I know that Everett Shockley, even after he was no longer Commonwealth Attorney for Pulaski County, continued to attend parole hearings and to argue against Epperly's release.

Eight years after the Epperly trial, I was elected Clerk of the Circuit Court of Pulaski County and served in the capacity until becoming a judge in 2006. During my 18 years as Clerk of Court, I received many letters from Steve Epperly in which he requested copies of various documents from his court file. I routinely sent him what he requested with a note inquiring about his well-being.

Sometime during the 1990's, I became concerned about Epperly's spiritual health. Consequently, I asked Larry Lindsey, a friend from my church, to ride with me to Keen

Mountain Correctional Center in Oakwood, Buchanan County, Virginia, to visit Epperly.

Following a security check, the guards took us to a meeting room to see Epperly. After a discussion about prison life, I gave Epperly a copy of Charles Colson's book, *Born Again*. He assured me that he would read it as Larry and I departed.

Shortly, after we began our descent from Keen Mountain Prison on our relatively long drive back to Pulaski County, Larry looked over at me from the passenger seat with an expression unlike any I had seen on his face before. He said very emphatically, "That guy's exactly where he needs to be!" I suppose I had spent so much time with Steve Epperly during the year of 1980, that his aberrant behavior did not seem unusual to me.

As I was completing this final Chapter, I read the June 28, 2015, Sunday Edition of *The Southwest Times*, the Pulaski newspaper. The front page story read, "After 35 Years Gina's Not Been Forgotten." The memories engendered by my involvement in this case will surely live on in my consciousness for the rest of my life.

"That's Incredible" producer Mark Grossan (left) confers with Radford Police, Pulaski Commonwealth's Attorney Everett Shockley and dog trainer John Preston.
Credit: The Roanoke Times.

Epilogue

In the past thirty-five years, Stephen Epperly has been incarcerated in several different Virginia correctional facilities and, at this writing, he is imprisoned at the Buckingham correctional unit.

Recently, I was holding court in a far southwestern Virginia county. When there was a lull in the courtroom, one of the bailiffs told me that he had been a guard at Keen Mountain Correctional Center when Epperly was a prisoner at that facility. He related to me that one day Epperly came into the prison yard to use a telephone booth which was accessible to the inmates. Another prisoner was using the phone at the time. So Epperly picked up the booth and slammed it, along with its occupant, to the ground.

Similar stories have made their way back to Pulaski County over the years. How much they have been embellished is not known.

Several years after the trial, Carl Gregory, an old family friend, told me that he was fishing below the Claytor Lake Dam on the night Gina Hall went missing. The Davis cabin was near the top of the dam. Carl related to me that sometime after one a.m. he heard a motorboat engine start and the sound faded into the distance. About an hour later, he heard the sound of an engine becoming louder as it neared the dam. The engine then became silent. Who knows whether or not the sounds that Carl heard that night had anything to do with the disappearance of Gina Hall.

One final note about my involvement in the Epperly case. Many people have asked me why I represented Stephen Epperly and if I believed he was guilty. These questions have always taken me aback. I have assumed (albeit wrongly) that everyone knows how the American system of justice works. Whether a person is guilty or innocent has nothing to do with his or her constitutional right to a fair trial and to competent counsel. It is up to the trier(s) of fact (judge and/or jury) to make the final decision based upon admissible evidence. If everyone does his part well, the principles of our Founding Fathers are vindicated.

Acknowledgements

There are many people I wish to thank for helping to make this book a reality. My wife, Jane, has been a willing and able sounding board and has consistently provided me with "one more idea" to improve the book's content. My former law partner, David Warburton, has been kind enough to meet with me and discuss the events surrounding the *Epperly* case, insuring to some degree that my memories have not become totally distorted through the passage of thirty-five years.

Maetta Crewe, Clerk of the Pulaski County Circuit court, has exhibited great patience and helpfulness in providing copies of the documents contained in the official court casefile. Ramona Palmer, who was our legal assistant in 1980, has reinforced my memories of events and encouraged me with her ever-present sense of humor. Cheryl Ashworth not only typed the first drafts but did some editing as well. My sister, Julia Lookabill Oravecz, a retired high school English teacher, was very helpful to her kid brother in suggesting more effective words and phrases.

Since this is my first foray into the book-writing arena, I would like to thank the publisher, Tom Perry, of Laurel Hill Publishing for his invaluable practical insights and helpful suggestions about the cover, the layout and even the content. Tom and I would like to thank Kathy Kiser Valencic for putting us together on this book.

About the Author

Royce Glennwood "Woody" Lookabill was born in Pulaski, Virginia. He graduated from Pulaski High School, The College of William and Mary, and Washington and Lee University School of Law. After graduating from college, he served in the United States Army for two years before entering law school.

The author served as law clerk for the late Justice Alex M. Harman, Jr., of the Supreme Court of Virginia, as Assistant Commonwealth Attorney for Pulaski County, as a general practitioner of the law, and as Clerk of the Pulaski County Circuit Court. Since 2006, he has served as a judge in the General District Courts of the 27th Judicial District.

Woody and his wife Jane have been married for 43 years and reside in Draper, Virginia. They are the parents of Kimberly, Joshua, and David and the grandparents of Olivia, Jude, Naomi, Adelaide, Emma, and Emersyn.

Index

H

habeas corpus, 44, 64, 68, 71, 73
  Hall, Gina, 2, 12, 24, 25, 26, 28, 34, 35, 36, 37,8, 14, 15, 30, 35, 36, 41, 42, 43, 45, 46, 47, 48, 49, 58, 62, 64, 72, 78
Harass II, 6, 43
Hazel Hollow, 15, 26, 36, 37, 40, 45

J

Jenkins, 63, 67, 68
Judge Arthur, 10, 17, 24, 36, 43, 49, 55, 63
jury, 7, 8, 9, 13, 14, 18, 27, 28, 29, 30, 31, 33, 35, 40, 42, 43, 45, 48, 49, 56, 59, 60, 61, 63, 65, 71, 72, 78, 26, 34, 36, 46, 54,

K

Keen Mountain, 74, 77
King, 35, 37, 38
Kulp, 68, 70

L

Lindsey, 73
Lookabill, 2, 3, 4, 9, 40, 72, 79, 81

M

Marriott, 35
McClung, 22
Monte Carlo, 15, 35, 36, 37, 45, 46, 58
Mottesheard, 52

N

Neeley, 67
Neely, 63
New River, 15, 16, 20, 26, 37, 41, 45, 46, 58

P

Palmer, 52, 79
Patton, 15
Pepper's Ferry, 20
Poff, 71
Preston, 6, 42, 43, 66, 76
Prices Fork, 20, 35
Pulaski County Circuit Court, 10, 18, 23, 63, 81
Pulaski County Courthouse, 20, 21
Pulaski County Grand Jury, 2, 48, 56
Pulaski County High School, 19
Pulaski County Sheriff's Department, 10, 46

R

Radford Arsenal, 20

Radford University, 2, 14, 19, 35

Richmond, Virginia, 67

Roanoke, Virginia, 14, 40, 51, 54, 69, 72, 76

Roanoke Times, 14, 40, 54, 72, 76

Ross, 46

Rules of Court for Criminal Procedure, 23

Rules of Court for Criminal Proceedings, 56

Russell, 40, 67

S

Saltzburg, 69

Shockley, 17, 27, 34, 40, 41, 45, 51, 55, 56, 60, 61, 73, 76

Stewart, 12

Supreme Court of Virginia, 24, 29, 44, 61, 63, 67, 68, 71, 81

T

That's a damn good dog, 3, 47

The Southwest Times, 6, 12, 16, 26, 58, 66, 74

U

United States District Court for the Western District of Virginia, 68

University of Virginia Law School, 69

V

Valencic, 80

Virginia Rules of Court, 27

Virginia State Penitentiary, 63

Virginia Tech, 2, 18, 20, 57

voir dire, 29, 30, 31

W

Warburton, 2, 8, 9, 34, 40, 43, 67, 79

WBDJ, 2, 62

WDBJ, 51

West End, 19, 36, 43, 45

West End Radford, 19, 36, 43

Writ of Prohibition, 24

Made in the USA
Middletown, DE
19 April 2016